WORDS
LIFE OR DEATH

ROBERT MORRIS

STUDY GUIDE

GATEWAY PRESS

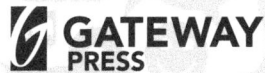

Words: Life or Death Study Guide
Copyright © 2018 by Robert Morris

Content taken from sermons delivered in 2012 by Robert Morris at Gateway Church, Southlake, Texas.

Unless otherwise noted, Scripture quotations taken from the New King James Version®. Copyright © 1982 by Thomas Nelson. Used by permission. All rights reserved.

Scripture quotations marked (NIV) are taken from the Holy Bible, New International Version®, NIV®. Copyright © 1973, 1978, 1984, 2011 by Biblica, Inc.™ Used by permission of Zondervan. All rights reserved worldwide. www.zondervan.com. The "NIV" and "New International Version" are trademarks registered in the United States Patent and Trademark Office by Biblica, Inc.™

Scripture quotations marked (NLT) are taken from the Holy Bible, New Living Translation, copyright ©1996, 2004, 2015 by Tyndale House Foundation. Used by permission of Tyndale House Publishers, Inc., Carol Stream, Illinois 60188. All rights reserved.

All rights reserved. No portion of this publication may be reproduced, stored in a retrieval system, or transmitted in any form by any means—electronic, mechanical, photocopying, recording, or any other—without prior permission from the publisher.

ISBN: 978-1-945529-56-6

We hope you hear from the Holy Spirit and receive God's richest blessings from this book by Gateway Press. We want to provide the highest quality resources that take the messages, music, and media of Gateway Church to the world. For more information on other resources from Gateway Publishing, go to gatewaypublishing.com.

Gateway Press, an imprint of Gateway Publishing
700 Blessed Way
Southlake, Texas 76092
gatewaypublishing.com

18 19 20 21 22   7 6 5 4 3 2 1
Printed in the United States of America

CONTENTS

SESSION **1**	The Value of Words	1
SESSION **2**	The Truth About Words	11
SESSION **3**	Ten Deadly Sins	21
SESSION **4**	Amazing Facts	35
SESSION **5**	Bridling the Tongue	47
SESSION **6**	The Pure Language	59
SESSION **7**	Receiving the Holy Spirit	71
	Leader's Guide	85

1

THE VALUE OF WORDS

Our quality of life is dependent on our words because our words determine how we connect with God and others.

ENGAGE
Do you think the words you speak have any real value? Why or why not?

WATCH
Watch "The Value of Words."
- Listen to how our words shape the way our lives develop.
- Watch for the key to using your words to improve relationships.

(If you are not able to watch this teaching on video, read the following. Otherwise, skip to the **Talk** section after viewing.)

READ

The quality of your life depends on the words you speak.

If this wasn't in the Bible, I wouldn't believe it myself. I realize it is very difficult to think of our mouths as having this much power. However, the Bible tells us:

> A man's stomach shall be satisfied from the fruit of his mouth;
> *From* the produce of his lips he shall be filled.
> Death and life *are* in the power of the tongue,
> And those who love it will eat its fruit (Proverbs 18:20-21).

God created by speaking. He did not "think" light into existence; He **said**, "Let there be light!" (Genesis 1:3). We are made in God's image, so there is something about *speaking* that is a creative force in our lives. Now, this truth has been distorted by the enemy and turned into a "name it and claim it" motto for some. However, this isn't about getting God to agree with our words. We need to get our words into agreement with God. That's what makes the difference in our quality of life—agreeing with God's plan, not Satan's.

Words Connect Us to God

Words are how God connects the spiritual realm where He lives to the natural realm where we live. The Gospel of John teaches us that Jesus is the Word:

The Value of Words

> The Word became flesh and dwelt among us, and we beheld His glory, the glory as of the only begotten of the Father, full of grace and truth (John 1:14).

There was a chasm between God and us called sin, and God sent His Word to span that chasm.

In the same way, we use our words to connect with God. Romans 10:9 says if we believe something in our hearts, we must speak words that agree with this belief. We confess (or speak) Jesus is Lord, and this confession is the bridge that unites us with the Father.

What we really believe in our hearts will come out of our mouths. Jesus said,

> "Therefore I say to you, every sin and blasphemy will be forgiven men, but the blasphemy *against* the Spirit will not be forgiven men. Anyone who speaks a word against the Son of Man, it will be forgiven him; but whoever speaks against the Holy Spirit, it will not be forgiven him, either in this age or in the *age* to come. Either make the tree good and its fruit good, or else make the tree bad and its fruit bad; for a tree is known by *its* fruit. Brood of vipers! How can you, being evil, speak good things? For out of the abundance of the heart the mouth speaks. A good man out of the good treasure of his heart brings forth good things, and an evil man out of the evil treasure brings forth evil things. But I say to you that for every idle word men may speak, they

will give account of it in the day of judgment. For by your words you will be justified, and by your words you will be condemned" (Matthew 12:31–37).

The enemy often uses this passage to condemn believers, attempting to convince them they have committed the unpardonable sin. However, if you had committed blasphemy against the Holy Spirit, your heart would be too hardened to have any interest in this message. In fact, your heart would be too hardened to seek God at all. Blasphemy against the Holy Spirit is a sin of words, but it begins in the heart. Jesus ministered through the power of the Holy Spirit, but the Pharisees and religious leaders attributed these works to the devil. Jesus warned that they were moving toward blasphemy—a heart so far away from God that it gives His glory to the enemy.

By studying this series together, none of us are guilty of blasphemy. However, we should all examine our hearts. The words we speak are the result of what we have treasured in our hearts.

Words Connect Us to Each Other

Words connect us not only to God but also to each other. Some people may find themselves in a disconnected marriage. The marriage we experience is typically the marriage we have created with our words. This isn't to say we have creative power equal to God's, but our words either agree with His plan for our lives or with the enemy's plan.

A great way to examine your marriage (or any relationship) is to read Ephesians 5:25-26:

> Husbands, love your wives, just as Christ also loved the church and gave Himself for her, that He might sanctify and cleanse her with the washing of water by the word.

Are you cleansing your spouse with the words you speak to and about them? Or do you find yourself constantly focused on their negative qualities? You may be thinking to yourself, "Well, they only have *one* good quality." That's okay; focus on that one thing. If all they do well is get up in the morning, tell them daily that they are the best "getter-upper" around! Quit using your words to speak death over the different areas of your life. Hurtful and negative words have opened the door to the enemy, and we need to use positive, life-giving words to close this door and bring healing to our relationships.

NOTES

_____

_____

_____

_____

_____

TALK

These questions can be used for group discussion or personal reflection.

Question 1

Why does the quality of your life depend on the words you speak?

_____

_____

_____

_____

Question 2

Read Romans 10:9. Why does salvation involve your mouth and not just your heart?

_____

_____

_____

_____

Question 3

Do you find it easy to speak life over others? Why or why not?

_____

_____

Question 4
Read Proverbs 8:8. What areas of your speech lack righteousness?

_____

_____

_____

Question 5
Seven key words to healing any relationship are, "I was wrong. Will you forgive me?" Who needs to hear these words from you today?

_____

_____

_____

_____

PRAY

If studying alone, ask the Holy Spirit to reveal the truth about Himself to you. If in a group, take some time to pray for each other as you think about the truths discussed in this session.

EXPLORE

Do you want to go deeper with this teaching? Here are some additional things to think about, pray for, or write about in your journal throughout the next week.

Key Thought

> *Our words either agree with God's plan for our life, or they agree with Satan's plan for our life. Every word we speak is either releasing life or releasing death in our lives.*

In what areas or relationships have your words released death instead of life?

_____

_____

_____

_____

_____

The Value of Words | 9

Key Verses
Proverbs 18:20-21; Matthew 12:31-37
　　What truths stand out to you as you read these verses?

_____

_____

_____

　　What is the Holy Spirit saying to you through these Scriptures?

_____

_____

_____

Key Question
Ephesians 5 teaches us how Jesus gently cleanses us with words. Who needs to be gently washed by your words today?

Key Prayer
　　Heavenly Father, thank You for the gift of Your Word, Jesus, who came to save and heal us. I surrender my heart to Your Holy Spirit. Teach me to use my words to connect with You and others in a fruitful way. In Jesus' name, Amen.

2

THE TRUTH ABOUT WORDS

If grace has come into your life, your heart will be changed. If your heart has been changed, your mouth will be changed too.

RECAP

In the previous session, we discussed how words affect our quality of life. We also learned how our words connect us to God and each other. Our words are evidence of what is really in our hearts. We must choose to speak life over our relationships and train our mouths to agree with God's plan.

Did you find any new opportunities to speak life over the people around you this week?

> ### ENGAGE
> Share a quote from your favorite childhood movie or television show.
>
> ### WATCH
> Watch "The Truth About Words."
> - Think about situations in which hurtful words can leave lasting wounds.
> - Listen for the lies we believe about our words and the truth that can set us free.
>
> (If you are not able to watch this teaching on video, read the following. Otherwise, skip to the **Talk** section after viewing.)

READ

In Matthew 12:33, Jesus speaks to the Pharisees about their words using this analogy:

> "Either make the tree good and its fruit good, or else make the tree bad and its fruit bad; for a tree is known by *its* fruit."

The tree represents the heart, and the fruit is the mouth. Jesus goes on to say in verses 34-37 that words reveal what is in a man's heart, and men will one day give an account of every word they speak. People who have experienced God's grace have a true heart change, and this should be reflected in the way they speak.

Words Cost

Can a person speak freely? The answer may surprise you. The truth is words are never free; they always cost us something. As Americans, we are blessed to live in a country with the right to freedom of speech; however, this right does not mean we have no accountability for our words. We're accountable to God for every word we speak (Matthew 12:36-37) because God's law is higher than any law of man.

When we speak hurtful words over someone, the cost can be diminished trust, decreased intimacy, or even the loss of the relationship itself. Psalm 141:3 says, "Set a guard, O Lord, over my mouth; keep watch over the door of my lips." In Psalm 39:1, King David demonstrates just how important words are:

> I said, "I will guard my ways,
> Lest I sin with my tongue;
> I will restrain my mouth with a muzzle."

Have you ever made the statement, "I probably shouldn't say this …" but then said whatever it was you should not have said? This warning is usually the Holy Spirit or common sense (or both) telling us not to say something, and yet we do it anyway. Sarcasm is very prevalent in today's movies and television shows, but when we are sarcastic in our speech, we often find ourselves hurting others.

Words Hurt

Do words still hurt even if you are joking? Yes. We often try to convince ourselves that humor removes the sting of hurtful words, but this is simply not true. Proverbs 26:18-19 says:

> Like a madman who throws firebrands, arrows, and death,
> *Is* the man *who* deceives his neighbor,
> And says, "I was only joking!"

We often use verbal "jabs" or hints in our comments, and if we receive a jab, we are quick to "stab" in return. We search for a person's weakness to exploit with our words. Then, if the person objects, we defensively reply, "I was just kidding" or "You are too sensitive." We may argue, "I didn't mean anything by that," but the Bible disagrees. Matthew 12:34 says, "Out of the abundance of the heart the mouth speaks." In other words, if something comes out of your mouth, it's because it is in your heart.

When evil words come out of your mouth, it's an opportunity to examine your heart. Ask God to show you the root of your words and how you should deal with it. Repent and ask for forgiveness. Perhaps you have been the recipient of hurtful words. The only way to break free of them is to forgive the person who said them.

Words Last

Words do not evaporate or disappear. On the contrary, James 3:5-6 says the tongue can start a forest fire. Your hurtful words can add to wounds a person already has and stay with them a long time. Marriage relationships can be destroyed when one partner continuously uses words to cut the other down. Hurtful words don't disappear, but they can and do damage the people around us.

The good news is good words last as well. In 2 Timothy 1, the apostle Paul says he "remembers" Timothy in his prayers. The word "remember" in this passage refers to a graveyard monument. This object serves to remind others not that a person has died but rather that a person has lived. Paul is saying he is building a monument of Timothy's need before God. We may not always see the answers to our prayers right away, but we can rest assured that our prayers have no expiration date before God.

Bad words cost, but good words can be an investment. Bad words hurt, but good words can heal. Bad words last, but thankfully, good words do too.

NOTES

_____

_____

_____

_____

_____

TALK

These questions can be used for group discussion or personal reflection.

Question 1

As a believer, do you have the "right" to say whatever you want? Why or why not?

Question 2

Read Romans 12:17-18. How should you respond when someone speaks hurtful words over you? How is this different from your natural response?

Question 3
Read Matthew 12:34. When your words reveal bad fruit in your heart, what should you do?

_____

_____

_____

Question 4
Have your words ever put a chasm between you and a family member or friend? How did you attempt to resolve the situation?

_____

_____

_____

_____

Question 5
Read Proverbs 12:25. What person in your life could use a "good word" today?

_____

_____

_____

_____

PRAY

If studying alone, ask the Holy Spirit to reveal the truth about Himself to you. If in a group, take some time to pray for each other as you think about the truths discussed in this session.

EXPLORE

Do you want to go deeper with this teaching? Here are some additional things to think about, pray for, or write about in your journal throughout the next week.

Key Thought

If we speak words that hurt someone, it will cost us something in that relationship. The good news is that our words can also be an investment in someone that builds them up instead of tearing them down.

How careful are you with your words? Do you use your speech to tear others down, or do you speak words of life into your relationships?

_____

_____

_____

_____

_____

Key Verses
Matthew 12:33-37; Proverbs 18:21; 2 Timothy 1:3, 5

    What truths stand out to you as you read these verses?

_____

_____

_____

    What is the Holy Spirit saying to you through these Scriptures?

_____

_____

_____

Key Question
Understanding the impact your words have on every relationship, what do you need to work on to improve your communication with others?

Key Prayer
> *Father, I ask You to forgive me for the times I have used my words carelessly or hurtfully. Please reveal the root of any hurt in my heart and show me any areas of unforgiveness I have toward others. Help me use my mouth to bless You and others. In Jesus' name, Amen.*

3

TEN DEADLY SINS

When we sin with our mouths, we separate ourselves from God and prevent Him from working in our lives the way He desires.

RECAP

In the previous session, we discovered the truth about words. We learned that hurtful words can have long-lasting and damaging effects on relationships. Words reflect the heart, and when we use hurtful words, we need to examine our hearts to find the root of the problem. When used correctly, words can invest, heal, and have eternal significance.

In the past week, have you noticed yourself choosing your words more carefully?

> ## ENGAGE
> What are your top three favorite sports teams?
> ## WATCH
> Watch "Ten Deadly Sins."
> - Consider how common these sins are in your daily life.
> - Remember the grace of God and the power of the Holy Spirit at work in you.
>
> (If you are not able to watch this teaching on video, read the following. Otherwise, skip to the **Talk** section after viewing.)

READ

Proverbs 18:21 says, "Death and life *are* in the power of the tongue." The sins we commit with our mouths produce death rather than life. These sins separate us from God and keep Him from being able to work in our lives the way He desires. The prophet Isaiah explains it this way:

> Behold, the Lord's hand is not shortened,
> That it cannot save;
> Nor His ear heavy,
> That it cannot hear.
> But your iniquities have separated you from your God;
> And your sins have hidden *His* face from you,
> So that He will not hear.
> For your hands are defiled with blood,

And your fingers with iniquity;
Your lips have spoken lies,
Your tongue has muttered perversity (Isaiah 59:1-3).

This passage does not say God cannot hear, but rather that He *will not*. There is nothing wrong with God; the problem is with sin. When we sin through our words or actions, we cut ourselves off from intimacy with God.

Lying

Proverbs 6:16-19 says:

These six *things* the Lord hates,
Yes, seven *are* an abomination to Him:
A proud look,
A lying tongue,
Hands that shed innocent blood,
A heart that devises wicked plans,
Feet that are swift in running to evil,
A false witness *who* speaks lies,
And one who sows discord among brethren.

God doesn't just love truth—He **is** truth. Proverbs 12:22 tells us, "Lying lips *are* an abomination to the Lord, but those who deal truthfully *are* His delight." *Abomination* is a very strong word for sin and means "detestable." The seven behaviors listed above are idolatrous to the Lord. When we lie, we leave the throne of truth and go to the throne of lies. Lying is detestable to God because it is opposite of His nature. When we speak something that is untrue, we are speaking completely against the nature of God.

A bad *stronghold* is a habit you can't break—something you do over and over again. There is a remedy, though, and it applies to all 10 deadly sins. To break a bad stronghold, you must become both accountable **and** correctable. Accountability will not lead to change unless you are willing to accept correction.

Sowing Discord

> A worthless person, a wicked man,
> Walks with a perverse mouth;
> He winks with his eyes,
> He shuffles his feet,
> He points with his fingers;
> Perversity *is* in his heart,
> He devises evil continually,
> He sows discord.
> Therefore his calamity shall come suddenly;
> Suddenly he shall be broken without remedy (Proverbs 6:12-15).

Our works come from our words. If we fix our words, we will fix our works. People who sow discord will reap calamity. When you speak disharmony and disunity, you will reap disharmony and disunity in your own life, and it will come suddenly and in a calamitous way. One of the ways we unknowingly do this is when a person complains to us about his or her spouse. Do we try to bring unity to their marriage? If not, we are sowing discord.

Gossip

Gossip is spreading intimate or private rumors or facts. Notice that gossip does not only apply to rumors. Even if a private matter is a fact, sharing it with others is still gossip. Proverbs 20:19 says, "A gossip tells secrets, so don't hang around with someone who talks too much" (NLT).

In 2 Corinthians 12:20, the apostle Paul tells the Corinthian church:

> For I am afraid that when I come to visit you I won't like what I find, and then you won't like my response. I am afraid that I will find quarreling, jealousy, outbursts of anger, selfishness, backstabbing, gossip, conceit, and disorderly behavior (NLT).

In the church, we often disguise gossip by calling it a "prayer request." The problem is we're doing more talking than praying. The next time you start to "share" something, ask yourself, "Am I really burdened for this person? Is my heart broken for this person like God's heart is?" Don't get excited when you hear the words, "Did you hear?" Get in a habit of not listening to or spreading gossip.

Slander

Slander is a false and malicious statement or report about someone. We often repeat reports without having personal knowledge of the truth. Whether we get our "information" from a person, the internet, or another source, we can slander others without even realizing it!

Scripture is clear about God's position on slander:

> Let not a slanderer be established in the earth;
> Let evil hunt the violent man to overthrow *him* (Psalm 140:11).

Proverbs 10:18 says a person who slanders is a fool, and Paul instructs believers not to associate with anyone who calls themselves a Christian but is a slanderer (1 Corinthians 5:11 NIV).

Christians sometimes spread bad reports about other churches, even though we are on the same team. We all have one goal: trying to win people to Jesus Christ. Stop speaking bad reports about others and start striving to be known for your gracious speech.

Tale-Bearing

Tale-bearing means revealing secrets or breaking a confidence.

> A talebearer reveals secrets,
> But he who is of a faithful spirit conceals a matter (Proverbs 11:13).

The church should be the safest place to reveal the secrets of our lives. We confess our faults to God to be forgiven, but James 5:16 instructs us to confess our faults to each other to be healed. How many forgiven people do we have in the church who are not healed? And how many unhealed people are not confessing their faults to one another because they tried before and the information was spread all over the church?

Knowing something about someone gives you power. *Character* is having power and using it wisely. Many believers will never have power because they do not have the character to use it wisely.

Cursing

Paul writes to the people of Rome:

"Their throat *is* an open tomb;
With their tongues they have practiced deceit";
"The poison of asps *is* under their lips";
"Whose mouth *is* full of cursing and bitterness" (Romans 3:13-14).

When you curse, you are speaking a curse. We are to bless, not curse. Why would you curse someone else? Why would you curse your marriage or your business? One of the most common curses spoken in our society is to *damn*, which comes from the word "damnation," meaning eternal condemnation. Why would we ever damn someone? Our marriages? Our checkbooks? Psalm 109:17-18 says cursing and blessing do not mix. A person who curses is not blessed.

Blasphemy

Blasphemy means to use God's name in an unsacred or self-serving way. The third commandment says:

> "You shall not take the name of the Lord your God in vain, for the Lord will not hold *him* guiltless who takes His name in vain" (Exodus 20:7).

There are two ways to take God's name in vain: to use God's name as a curse word and to use God's name in a vain (self-serving) way. Believers are often guilty of this second way because they say "God told me this" in an effort to manipulate others. We should never use God's name to get our way—that is blasphemy.

Filthy Language

We already talked about cursing, but filthy language is a different problem.

> But now you yourselves are to put off all these: anger, wrath, malice, blasphemy, filthy language out of your mouth (Colossians 3:8).

Filthy language comes out of your mouth because it is in your heart. It stirs up lust and leads to unhealthy and unclean thoughts.

Contentious Speech

Contentious speech is hurtful, hateful, malicious, disagreeable, or argumentative speech.

> Better to dwell in a corner of a housetop,
> Than in a house shared with a contentious woman (Proverbs 21:9).

Proverbs 26:21 teaches us that contentious speech is like adding wood to a fire. Some people love to argue or stir up strife. They think it is fun, but they fail to realize they are developing a contentious spirit. A contentious spirit drives people away because no one wants to spend time with a person who always has to have the last word.

Unbelief

Unbelief is a sin you commit with your mouth. Remember, what is in your heart will come out of your mouth. Unbelief can also be called "negativity." Negative words are words of unbelief.

> Beware, brethren, lest there be in any of you an evil heart of unbelief in departing from the living God; but exhort one another daily, while it is called "Today," lest any of you be hardened through the deceitfulness of sin (Hebrews 3:12-13).

Remember the story of the 12 spies in the Old Testament? Ten of them came back with a negative report, which God considered unbelief. The other two, though, came back with a positive report. The Bible calls this "faith." Faith is not refusing to see the mountain; rather, it is seeing the mountain *and* the Mountain-Mover! The two spies who gave the positive report were not delusional. They saw the same giants the other spies saw, but they knew their God was bigger.

Why did God put giants in the Promised Land? So no one could ever take the land without Him. The only way God could bless His children was to get their mouths to line up with His Word. The same is true for us today. We must stop speaking curses and start speaking blessings.

NOTES

_____
_____
_____
_____
_____
_____

TALK

These questions can be used for group discussion or personal reflection.

Question 1

If God is omnipresent, why does Isaiah 59 say He *will not* hear our prayers when we sin?

_____

_____

_____

_____

Question 2

According to this message, what is the definition of *character*? How do people of character react when it comes to gossip, slander, and tale bearing?

_____

_____

_____

_____

Question 3
Read Proverbs 12:22. Why is lying detestable to God?

_____
_____
_____
_____

Question 4
Read Exodus 20:7. Why is it dangerous to try to manipulate others by saying, "God told me this ..."?

_____
_____
_____
_____

Question 5
What are the two keys to tearing down strongholds?

_____
_____
_____
_____

PRAY

If studying alone, ask the Holy Spirit to reveal the truth about Himself to you. If in a group, take some time to pray for each other as you think about the truths discussed in this session.

EXPLORE

Do you want to go deeper with this teaching? Here are some additional things to think about, pray for, or write about in your journal throughout the next week.

Key Thought
> *Character is having power and using it wisely. This is why many believers will never have power—because they don't have the character to use it wisely.*

If the church is going to be a safe place for people to confess their faults, what changes do you need to make to become a more trustworthy person?

_____
_____
_____
_____
_____

Key Verses
Proverbs 6:12-19; Proverbs 12:22; Romans 3:13-14; Isaiah 59:1-3; Proverbs 26:21; Exodus 20:7

What truths stand out to you as you read these verses?

_____

_____

_____

What is the Holy Spirit saying to you through these Scriptures?

_____

_____

_____

Key Question
Do any of these 10 sins have a stronghold in your life, and if so, what godly, trustworthy person will you ask to help you be accountable and correctable?

Key Prayer
Heavenly Father, thank You for Your amazing grace. I repent for sinning with my mouth and allowing my words to separate me from You. Holy Spirit, please convict me whenever my mouth does not line up with God's Word. I want to be a person of character who shows Your love through both my actions and the words I speak. In Jesus' name, Amen.

4

AMAZING FACTS

The tongue is humanly untamable but divinely tamable.
The One who made it can tame it.

RECAP

In the previous session, we discussed the 10 deadly sins we commit with our mouths. These sins not only speak death into our lives but they also create distance between God and us.

Did you find yourself more aware of the Holy Spirit's conviction about the words of your mouth this week?

> ## ENGAGE
> We all have facts that fascinate us. What is one random fact you enjoy sharing with others?
>
> ## WATCH
> Watch "Amazing Facts."
> - Consider how the tongue is like a bit, a rudder, and a spark.
> - Listen for the good news about the tongue.
>
> (If you are not able to watch this teaching on video, read the following. Otherwise, skip to the **Talk** section after viewing.)

READ

James 3:1-12 is the longest discourse on the tongue in the Bible. It begins:

> My brethren, let not many of you become teachers, knowing that we shall receive a stricter judgment. For we all stumble in many things. If anyone does not stumble in word, he *is* a perfect man, able also to bridle the whole body (James 3:1-2).

According to these verses, anyone who can control his mouth can control his entire body. Think about the lusts of the flesh we all have dealt with in some way (food, sexual temptation, etc.). James says if you can get your tongue fixed, you can get your body fixed.

*The Tongue Is **Disproportionately** Powerful*

> Indeed, we put bits in horses' mouths that they may obey us, and we turn their whole body. Look also at ships: although they are so large and are driven by fierce winds, they are turned by a very small rudder wherever the pilot desires. Even so the tongue is a little member and boasts great things.
> See how great a forest a little fire kindles! (James 3:3-5).

Now, I could just say the tongue is "powerful," but that is not the amazing fact. The tongue is *disproportionately* powerful, meaning it is very small but has a very large effect.

James uses three analogies, the first being a bit in a horse's mouth. A bit is a very small piece of metal that controls the strength and direction of an animal that weighs 1,000-1,200 pounds, on average. In the same way, your tongue is a small body part, but it can control your strength and direction.

Many people take skills assessment tests to help them discover their strengths. However, no amount of self-discovery will help you if you can't control your tongue. The reason is you will not be able to direct your strengths in the right way. Without a bit, you cannot control a horse. Without a bridle on your tongue, you cannot control your body. James 1:26 says if you don't bridle your tongue, your service to God is useless.

The second analogy James uses is the rudder of a ship. A ship can be a very large vessel, but it is steered by one small, crucial piece: the rudder. Any captain will tell you that in a storm, a ship must face the right direction or else it will capsize. Similarly, many people's lives capsize because their tongue does not face them in the right direction in life's storms. Rudders are important in good weather too. Even on a clear, sunny day, a boat without a rudder can end up on the rocks. When everything is going well in your life, your tongue is still crucial for direction.

The final analogy is a little spark that ignites a huge forest fire. One careless spark off a cigarette can devastate hundreds of acres of trees. One careless word from the tongue can inflict the same type of damage on a person's heart.

The Tongue Is **Inherently** Evil

> And the tongue *is* a fire, a world of iniquity. The tongue is so set among our members that it defiles the whole body, and sets on fire the course of nature; and it is set on fire by hell. For every kind of beast and bird, of reptile and creature of the sea, is tamed and has been tamed by mankind. But no man can tame the tongue. *It is* an unruly evil, full of deadly poison (James 3:6-8).

We were born with an evil tongue. We don't have to teach children to be rude or say mean things; we have to teach them to say nice things. The default setting on the tongue is to destroy, and unless we change this setting, we will always do more damage than good.

Think back to junior high school. Did you have any physical differences, such as glasses or braces? If your appearance was different in any way, other students were going to comment unkindly on it. Why? Because the tongue is inherently evil.

The Tongue Is **Humanly** Untamable

> But no man can tame the tongue. *It is* an unruly evil, full of deadly poison (James 3:8).

No human, whether male or female, can tame the tongue. Only the One who made it can tame it. Yes, the tongue is *divinely* tamable.

Moses had a problem with his tongue before **and** after he met the Lord. In Exodus 4:10, he says,

> "Oh my Lord, I *am* not eloquent, neither before or since You have spoken to Your servant; but I *am* slow of speech and slow of ongue."

Isn't it comforting to know that heroes of the faith like Moses struggled with their tongues just like you and I do? God responds to Moses:

> "Who has made man's mouth? Or who makes the mute, the deaf, the seeing, or the blind? *Have* not I, the Lord? Now therefore, go,

and I will be with your mouth and teach you what you shall say" (Exodus 4:11-12).

In Acts 2, the first thing the Holy Spirit does for the believers on the Day of Pentecost is change their tongues. The only way you can change your tongue is to submit your tongue to the Holy Spirit. Isn't it amazing that there is so much controversy about this gift of the Holy Spirit? Who do you think is responsible for this confusion?

Hell wants to occupy your mouth. Satan can't hurt you, but he's trying to get you to turn your mouth against yourself. Every time you speak, you are agreeing with life and God or death and Satan.

*The Tongue Is **Contrastingly** Productive*

> With it we bless our God and Father, and with it we curse men, who have been made in the similitude of God. Out of the same mouth proceed blessing and cursing. My brethren, these things ought not to be so. Does a spring send forth fresh *water* and bitter from the same opening? Can a fig tree, my brethren, bear olives, or a grapevine bear figs? Thus no spring yields both salt water and fresh (James 3:9-12).

Nature can't even do what the tongue does. A fig tree cannot produce olives, and a grapevine cannot produce figs, but the tongue can bless and curse. It is contrastingly productive. We use our tongues to bless God and then curse people who are made in His image.

The tongue can do a lot of damage, but it can also do a lot of good. The tongue can curse, but it can also bless. You can bless your marriage and your finances. You can bless your children and your job. Yes, the tongue can destroy, but it can also produce good fruit.

NOTES

_____
_____
_____
_____
_____

TALK

These questions can be used for group discussion or personal reflection.

Question 1
Read James 3:5-6. Has someone ever said a careless word or phrase that started a "fire" in your life? Why did this have such an impact on you?

_____

_____

_____

_____

Question 2
According to James 1:26, why should you bridle your tongue?

_____

_____

_____

_____

Question 3
Why is a rudder important for ships in good weather? How does this relate to the tongue?

_____

_____

_____

_____

Question 4
Does becoming a Christian mean you will never have problems with your tongue again? Why or why not?

_____

_____

_____

_____

Question 5
Read James 3:9-10. Why is the enemy so interested in the words we speak?

_____

_____

_____

_____

PRAY

If studying alone, ask the Holy Spirit to reveal the truth about Himself to you. If in a group, take some time to pray for each other as you think about the truths discussed in this session.

EXPLORE

Do you want to go deeper with this teaching? Here are some additional things to think about, pray for, or write about in your journal throughout the next week.

Key Thought

The only way you can change your tongue is to submit it to the Holy Spirit.

How does the Holy Spirit affect the default setting for believers' tongues?

_____

_____

_____

_____

_____

Key Verses
James 3:1-12; Exodus 4:10-12
What truths stand out to you as you read these verses?

_____

_____

_____

What is the Holy Spirit saying to you through these Scriptures?

_____

_____

_____

Key Question
What areas of your life do you need to stop cursing and start blessing?

Key Prayer
Heavenly Father, I have tried and failed to control my tongue. Only You have the power to tame it. Holy Spirit, I submit my tongue to You and ask You to help me know the right things to declare over my life and others. Help me produce good fruit with the words I speak. In Jesus' name, Amen.

5

BRIDLING THE TONGUE

Only God can tame the tongue, but we have the responsibility to bridle it.

RECAP

In the previous session, we explored four amazing facts about the tongue. We learned it is disproportionately powerful, inherently evil, humanly untamable, and contrastingly productive.

Thinking about your conversations over the past week, did you notice how powerful your words are?

> ## ENGAGE
> Sometimes we act before we think. Describe a time when you acted too quickly and later wished you had thought a bit more.
>
> ## WATCH
> Watch "Bridling the Tongue."
> - Listen for the three keys to help you bridle your tongue.
> - Watch for the two different places our thoughts come from.
>
> (If you are not able to watch this teaching on video, read the following. Otherwise, skip to the **Talk** section after viewing.)

READ

If the tongue is humanly untamable, are we free from any responsibility regarding the words we speak? Or are we called to cooperate with God? According to James 1:26,

> If anyone among you thinks he is religious and does not bridle his tongue but deceives his own heart, this one's religion *is* useless.

"Religion" in this verse refers to a person's service to God. Unless someone bridles his tongue, his service to God is useless.

The soul is humanly unsavable. We can't save ourselves—only God can. However, we still have the responsibility to turn, repent, and put our faith in Jesus Christ. In the same way, the tongue is humanly untamable, but we still have the responsibility to bridle it.

When you put a bridle on a wild horse for the first time, does the horse instantly become tame? No, it takes time to tame a wild horse. It also takes time to tame the tongue, and our responsibility is to begin to bridle it.

Pause

The first step we need to take toward bridling the tongue is to *pause*. James 1:19 instructs us to "be swift to hear, slow to speak, [and] slow to wrath." If you have a problem with anger, you probably also have a problem with talking. If we are going to be slow to anger, we also need to be slow to speak. We need to *pause*. Learn to stop and not saying anything for a moment. Remember to **W.A.I.T.**—ask yourself, "**W**hy **a**m **I t**alking?"

If life and death are in the power of the tongue—and they are—then why do we speak so quickly? The book of Proverbs has three central themes: your morals, your money, and your mouth. If you've ever had a problem with any of these areas, Proverbs can help.

> Whoever guards his mouth and tongue
> Keeps his soul from troubles (Proverbs 21:23).

> In the multitude of words sin is not lacking,
> But he who restrains his lips *is* wise (Proverbs 10:19).

Yes, only God can tame the tongue, but it's our responsibility to guard our mouths and restrain our lips. We must put forth an effort!

> He who has knowledge spares his words,
> *And* a man of understanding is of a calm spirit.
> Even a fool is counted wise when he holds his peace;
> *When* he shuts his lips, *he is considered* perceptive
> (Proverbs 17:27-28).

Keeping your mouth shut can be difficult. You may need to write yourself reminders or even physically cover your mouth with your hand. Repeat to yourself, "Don't talk!"

Have you ever answered someone *before* they finished speaking? And then they replied, "That's not what I was going to say!" Proverbs 18:13 says, "He who answers a matter before he hears *it*, it *is* folly and shame to him." If you have a problem saying the wrong thing at the wrong time, try not saying anything at all.

Ponder

We need to *ponder* (or think) before we speak. How many times have you said something and later regretted it? Don't you wish you had taken a moment to think about it first?

There are three types of people in this world:

1. Those who think **before** they talk
2. Those who think **while** they talk
3. Those who think **after** they talk

(Actually, there may be a fourth group too—those who never think!)

Which type of person are you? Most people would admit they think *while* or *after* they talk, but we should strive to think *before* we talk. Thinking doesn't just come from the mind, though. Scripture teaches that we also think with our hearts. Proverbs 23:7 says, "For as he thinks in his heart, so *is* he." Luke 2:19 tells us that after the shepherds came to visit the newly born Jesus, Mary "kept all these things and pondered them in her heart." Hebrews 4:12 is often quoted as a reference to the power of the Bible, but look at what it says about the heart:

> For the word of God *is* living and powerful, and sharper than any two-edged sword, piercing even to the division of soul and spirit, and of joints and marrow, and is a discerner of the thoughts and intents of the heart.

Medical science is now beginning to understand that our hearts can think. Multiple heart-transplant patients have reported experiencing thoughts and dreams that were actually related to the donors' lives. For example, an eight-year-old girl received a heart transplant from a murdered child. The recipient had such detailed nightmares of the donor's murder that the police were able to arrest the killer who was later convicted.

If we will pause and ponder, we can think with our hearts and not just our minds. Wouldn't it be better to give someone an answer from the bottom of your heart than the top of your mind? How many times have we had to go back to someone and say,

"I'm sorry! I didn't mean that. That's not in my heart" because we answered them from our mind? Remember what Jesus said: "Out of the abundance of the heart his mouth speaks" (Luke 6:45).

When you get saved, you get a new heart. However, your mind is still in the process of being renewed by the Word of God. Let your converted heart tell your renewing mind what to say.

Pray

Isaiah 6:1–8 says:

> In the year that King Uzziah died, I saw the Lord sitting on a throne, high and lifted up, and the train of His *robe* filled the temple. Above it stood seraphim; each one had six wings: with two he covered his face, with two he covered his feet, and with two he flew. And one cried to another and said:
>
> "Holy, holy, holy *is* the Lord of hosts;
> The whole earth *is* full of His glory!"
>
> And the posts of the door were shaken by the voice of him who cried out, and the house was filled with smoke.
> So I said:
>
> "Woe *is* me, for I am undone!
> Because I *am* a man of unclean lips,
> And I dwell in the midst of a people of unclean lips;

For my eyes have seen the King,
The Lord of hosts."

Then one of the seraphim flew to me, having in his hand a live coal *which* he had taken with the tongs from the altar. And he touched my mouth *with it,* and said:

"Behold, this has touched your lips;
Your iniquity is taken away,
And your sin purged."

Also I heard the voice of the Lord, saying:

"Whom shall I send,
And who will go for Us?"

Then I said, "Here *am* I! Send me."

When Isaiah came into the presence of the Lord, the first thing he was convicted about was his mouth. Verse 5 explains, "I *am* a man of unclean lips, and I dwell in the midst of a people of unclean lips." Think about how unclean, vulgar, and sarcastic our speech is today. We need to begin every day by coming into the presence of God and confessing our faults and weaknesses to Him. We cannot help other people unless we first have our own encounter with God.

Are your words an area of struggle in which you cannot seem to get victory? Have you tried to control your tongue but failed over and over again? Now is the time to examine your heart and ask yourself this question: "Have I laid my insecurities on the cross?" You don't have the power to control your tongue, but God does. He wants to take a live coal from the altar, purify your mouth, and change your heart as only He can do.

NOTES

_____
_____
_____
_____
_____
_____

TALK

These questions can be used for group discussion or personal reflection.

Question 1
Read James 1:19. Why is it important to be "slow to speak"?

_____
_____
_____
_____

Question 2
Is your tendency to think before, while, or after you talk? Which method is most beneficial?

_____
_____
_____
_____

Question 3
Why should Christians let their hearts tell their minds what to say?

_____
_____

Question 4
Read Isaiah 6:5. When Isaiah entered God's presence, what was his first area of conviction? Can you relate to this conviction?

Question 5
Every person deals with insecurity from time to time. What insecurities do you need to lay on the cross today?

PRAY

If studying alone, ask the Holy Spirit to reveal the truth about Himself to you. If in a group, take some time to pray for each other as you think about the truths discussed in this session.

EXPLORE

Do you want to go deeper with this teaching? Here are some additional things to think about, pray for, or write about in your journal throughout the next week.

Key Thought
Let your converted heart tell your renewing mind what to say.

Do you find yourself speaking words that do not reflect what is in your heart? What steps can you take to ensure the words of your mouth reflect the thoughts of your heart?

_____
_____
_____
_____
_____

Key Verses
James 1:19, 26; Isaiah 6:1-8; Psalm 34:12-13; Proverbs 23:7
What truths stand out to you as you read these verses?

_____

_____

_____

What is the Holy Spirit saying to you through these Scriptures?

_____

_____

_____

Key Question
God designed us to think with our minds and our hearts. In what areas do you need to renew your mind and guard your heart?

Key Prayer
Heavenly Father, thank You for teaching me how to use my words wisely. I want to learn to think before I speak. Holy Spirit, please help me bridle my tongue. I surrender control over every part of my life to You. Thank You, Lord, for Your amazing grace that is transforming my heart and mind. In Jesus' name, Amen.

6

THE PURE LANGUAGE

Praying in the Spirit is a key to learning to speak in purity.

RECAP

In the previous session, we talked about our responsibility to bridle the tongue. Only God can tame the tongue, but we should pause, ponder, and pray before speaking. We need to spend time in God's presence every day so that our words can be a blessing to others.

Did you remind yourself to W.A.I.T. this past week? How did this advice affect your conversations?

> ### ENGAGE
> Every culture has its own unique stories and myths. Name some myths you believed as a child.
>
> ### WATCH
> Watch "The Pure Language."
> - Look for any myths you have believed about the Holy Spirit.
> - Ask yourself if you have been putting on every piece of the armor of God.
>
> (If you are not able to watch this teaching on video, read the following. Otherwise, skip to the **Talk** section after viewing.)

READ

We have been discussing the importance of our words, and now we are going to discover a key to learning to speak in purity.

> When the Day of Pentecost had fully come, they were all with one accord in one place. And suddenly there came a sound from heaven, as of a rushing mighty wind, and it filled the whole house where they were sitting. Then there appeared to them divided tongues, as of fire, and *one* sat upon each of them. And they were all filled with the Holy Spirit and began to speak with other tongues, as the Spirit gave them utterance (Acts 2:1-4).

There is a pure language every believer can speak. This is not an earthly language, but rather speaking in tongues. We may also refer to this as a prayer language.

It Is a **Language**

Speaking in tongues is not gibberish. It is an actual language. Acts 2:6 says those gathered in Jerusalem for Pentecost heard the disciples speaking in tongues and "were confused, because everyone heard them speak in his own language." The Greek word for language in this verse is *diálektos*, which means "dialect." Each person heard in his own dialect. According to the Bible, speaking in tongues is a language.

There are many myths about speaking in tongues. Here are three of the most common ones.

Myth #1: You start speaking it fluently the first day.

People often think the disciples spoke fluently in tongues on the Day of Pentecost. However, the Bible does not say they spoke fluently; it says the people *heard* fluently. That was the miracle.

We have been learning about taming and bridling the tongue. Isn't it amazing that the first thing the Holy Spirit changes when He comes is the tongue? And the disciples had to cooperate with Him.

Have you ever tried to learn a second language? No one speaks a new language fluently right from the start. You have to practice in order to grow in your ability to speak in that language. The same is true for babies. Babies don't start speaking fluently right away, and we actually think it's cute when they mispronounce words. Many people are nervous to begin speaking in tongues and worried they might not do it "right." However, just like earthly parents, our heavenly Father likes hearing us talk. If you want to pray in a prayer language, you can! It's not going to be fluent from the first day, and that's okay. Your Father will like it anyway.

Myth #2: You can't control it.

People worry they will suddenly enter a trance and start speaking in tongues. They fear losing control and embarrassing themselves. Think about the other gifts, though. If you have the gift of teaching, can you control it? Absolutely. You only teach when you feel led to teach. What about the gift of prophecy? Scripture tells us, "The spirits of the prophets are subject to the prophets" (1 Corinthians 4:32). If you can control one gift, you can control them all. Speaking in tongues is an act of your will to cooperate with the Holy Spirit.

Myth #3: It's just going to jump out of you someday.

We use the excuse, "If God sees fit, He will give it to me some time." Well, God *has* given you this gift! If you pray for the gift of giving, money is not going to fly out of your pocket and jump into the offering box. No, you have to make a conscious decision to give. The same is true for speaking in tongues. You have to be willing to open your mouth and speak.

THE PURE LANGUAGE | 63

It Is a Language of the **Spirit**

In 1 Corinthians 14:2, the apostle Paul teaches that when you speak in tongues, you are speaking in the spirit. Speaking in tongues is speaking to God, not men. If you want to understand prayer language, I suggest memorizing 1 Corinthians 14:14-15:

> For if I pray in a tongue, my spirit prays, but my understanding is unfruitful. What is *the conclusion* then? I will pray with the spirit, and I will also pray with the understanding. I will sing with the spirit, and I will also sing with the understanding.

When you pray in tongues, your spirit is praying. Is it possible that the spirit has more understanding about a situation than the mind does? How many prayers are not fulfilled because we only pray with our understanding? We are made up of three parts: spirit, soul, and body. How many people only pray soulish prayers? Paul told the Corinthian church, "I thank my God I speak with tongues more than you all" (1 Corinthians 14:18). If the greatest apostle who ever lived prayed in tongues, shouldn't we pray this way too? Paul clearly says, "Do not forbid to speak with tongues" (1 Corinthians 14:39), but there are entire theological persuasions that disobey this instruction.

You may not immediately speak in tongues when you are baptized in the Holy Spirit. It is possible to have a stronghold in your mind in this area, especially if you were taught incorrectly about this gift. Why is there so much controversy over speaking in tongues? It is because life and death are in the power of the tongue, and the enemy does not want you to submit your tongue to the Holy Spirit.

Many people do not realize that praying in the spirit is actually part of the armor of God.

> Take the helmet of salvation and the sword of the Spirit, which is the word of God. And **pray in the Spirit** on all occasions with all kinds of prayers and requests. With this in mind, be alert and always keep on praying for all the Lord's people (Ephesians 6:17-18 NIV, emphasis added).

Is it possible that you are losing some battles because you are not putting on the *full* armor of God? Praying in the spirit is like lifting weights. Can you image how strong you would be if you prayed in the spirit every day?

*It Is a **Pure** Language*

Genesis 11 tells the story of the tower of Babel. Verse 1 says, "Now the whole earth had one language and one speech." Is it possible this was a heavenly language passed down from God through Adam and Eve? The people try to build a tower to get to heaven, but God stops them. Why? According to Genesis 11:5-7, it is because they would have succeeded. God says, "We (referring to the Trinity) better take this language away because all things are possible with it." Is it possible that if you use this heavenly language, nothing you pray for will be withheld from you?

> "For then I will restore to the peoples a pure language,
> That they all may call on the name of the Lord,
> To serve Him with one accord" (Zephaniah 3:9).

What language is pure? What language has no profanity and brings people together in "one accord"? Acts 2:1 says, "When the Day of Pentecost had fully come, they were all with one accord in one place." God restored the pure language promised in Zephaniah on the Day of Pentecost. There is only one pure language, and you can begin speaking in it today.

Speaking in tongues is not about the sounds or the syllables. Don't worry about what you sound like. Just have the courage to try. Open your mouth and submit your tongue to the Holy Spirit. Make the choice to pray with your understanding *and* with your spirit every day.

NOTES

_____

_____

_____

_____

TALK

These questions can be used for group discussion or personal reflection.

Question 1
What myths have you believed about speaking in tongues?

_____

_____

_____

_____

Question 2
Read 1 Corinthians 14:14-17. What is the difference between praying with the understanding and praying with the spirit? Why is it important to do both?

_____

_____

_____

_____

Question 3
Read Ephesians 6:14-18. Why does Paul include praying in the spirit with the armor of God?

_____

_____

_____

_____

Question 4
Why did God confuse the language of the people at Babel in Genesis 11?

_____

_____

_____

_____

Question 5
Will a person who is baptized in the Holy Spirit always begin speaking in tongues right away? Why or why not?

_____

_____

_____

_____

PRAY

If studying alone, ask the Holy Spirit to reveal the truth about Himself to you. If in a group, take some time to pray for each other as you think about the truths discussed in this session.

EXPLORE

Do you want to go deeper with this teaching? Here are some additional things to think about, pray for, or write about in your journal throughout the next week

Key Thought

How many of your prayers are not really being fulfilled because you are only praying with your understanding? Is it possible that the Holy Spirit has more understanding than you have about the situation?

Jude 20 says to build yourself up "on your most holy faith, praying in the Holy Spirit." What areas of your life need building up?

_____

_____

_____

_____

The Pure Language | 69

Key Verses
Acts 2:1-4; 1 Corinthians 14:1-2, 14-15; Ephesians 6:10-18; Jude 20; Genesis 11:1-7

What truths stand out to you as you read these verses?

_____

_____

_____

What is the Holy Spirit saying to you through these Scriptures?

_____

_____

_____

Key Question
How will praying with your understanding and with your spirit help you bridle your tongue?

Key Prayer
Heavenly Father, I believe all Your gifts are good. I don't want to miss out on anything You have for me. Holy Spirit, I yield my tongue to You. Teach me to pray not just with my mind but with my spirit as well. Please show me any areas of doubt or wrong belief I have about speaking in tongues. Help me to trust You with every part of my life. In Jesus' name, Amen.

7

RECEIVING THE HOLY SPIRIT

There are three baptisms every believer needs to experience: blood, water, and Spirit.

RECAP

In the previous session, we talked about God's gift of speaking in tongues. We learned it is a real, pure language that allows our spirits to communicate directly with God. We also examined three common myths that keep people from embracing and growing in their prayer language.

Whether praying in tongues is new or familiar to you, did you find more opportunities to use your prayer language last week?

> **ENGAGE**
>
> What is the most memorable or exciting gift you have ever received?
>
> **WATCH**
>
> Watch "Receiving the Holy Spirit."
> - Consider the three baptisms and the significance of each one.
> - Watch for examples of Spirit baptism in both the Old and New Testaments.
>
> (If you are not able to watch this teaching on video, read the following. Otherwise, skip to the **Talk** section after viewing.)

READ

The Greek word for "baptize" is transliterated *baptizó* and means to immerse (to get completely wet). There are three baptisms every believer needs to experience: blood, water, and Spirit.

The Holy Spirit Baptizes Us in Christ

In 1 Corinthians 12:13, the apostle Paul writes:

> For by one Spirit we were all baptized into one body—whether Jews or Greeks, whether slaves or free—and have all been made to drink into one Spirit.

Jesus shed His blood to wash away our sins and reconcile us with the Father. When we get saved, the Holy Spirit baptizes us into Jesus.

Receiving The Holy Spirit | 73

We become part of the body of Christ and have eternal security and hope through our Savior. Because the Holy Spirit is doing the baptizing, salvation can also be called the baptism *of* the Holy Spirit.

The Disciple Baptizes Us in Water
Matthew 28:19 says,

> "Go therefore and make disciples of all the nations, baptizing them in the name of the Father and of the Son and of the Holy Spirit."

Water baptism is an outward demonstration of the internal covenant we make with God through salvation. It is publicly declaring our decision to follow Jesus. Water baptism doesn't require a pastor—just a disciple. Anyone who is a disciple of Christ can baptize another believer.

Jesus Baptizes Us in the Holy Spirit
This is the baptism *in* (or *with*) the Holy Spirit. People often confuse this with the baptism *of* the Holy Spirit, which is actually salvation. The third baptism occurs when Jesus immerses a believer in the power of the Holy Spirit. John the Baptist said,

> "I indeed baptize you with water unto repentance, but He who is coming after me is mightier than I, whose sandals I am not worthy to carry. **He** will baptize you **with** the **Holy Spirit** and fire" (Matthew 3:11, emphasis added).

The first and third baptisms are not the same event. They are both theologically and grammatically different:

- In 1 Corinthians 12:13, the baptism is performed *by the Holy Spirit* into Jesus.
- In Matthew 3:11, the baptism is performed *by Jesus* into the Holy Spirit and fire.

The baptism in the Holy Spirit is mentioned in every gospel. Matthew, Mark, and Luke—known together as the Synoptic Gospels—include details about Jesus' last year of earthly ministry. John, however, writes about all three years. There are only four events mentioned in all four books: the death, burial, and resurrection of Christ and the baptism in the Holy Spirit. In addition to Matthew 3:11 (listed above), John the Baptist's declaration appears in the following verses:

- "I indeed baptized you with water, but He will baptize you with the Holy Spirit" (Mark 1:8).
- "I indeed baptize you with water; but One mightier than I is coming, whose sandal strap I am not worthy to loose. He will baptize you with the Holy Spirit and fire" (Luke 3:16).
- "I did not know Him, but He who sent me to baptize with water said to me, 'Upon whom you see the Spirit descending, and remaining on Him, this is He who baptizes with the Holy Spirit'" (John 1:33).

Receiving The Holy Spirit | 75

The accounts in Mark 1 and John 1 tell of Jesus being baptized in water before receiving the baptism in the Holy Spirit. The Holy Spirit had previously descended on others but never remained on them. Jesus was the first person the Holy Spirit ever descended and remained on.

If Jesus needed the baptism in the Holy Spirit while on earth, we certainly do too. Jesus is our example. He did not need to be saved or "born again" because he was born right the first time. We were born sinners, but we are born again perfect children of God. We can never be perfect in our performance, but we are perfect in our position in Christ. Jesus did experience the other two baptisms (water and Spirit), and we need to experience them as well.

In Acts 1, Jesus gives final instructions to His disciples before ascending into heaven:

> And being assembled together with *them,* He commanded them not to depart from Jerusalem, but to wait for the Promise of the Father, "which," *He said,* "you have heard from Me; for John truly baptized with water, but you shall be baptized with the Holy Spirit not many days from now" (vv. 4-5).

The disciples waited, fasted, and prayed for 10 days. On the Day of Pentecost, the Promise (the Holy Spirit) appeared upon each of them as a tongue of fire, and "they were all filled with the Holy Spirit and began to speak with other tongues, as the Spirit gave them utterance" (Acts 2:4). The apostle Peter preached to the crowd and instructed them:

> "Repent, and let every one of you be baptized in the name of Jesus Christ for the remission of sins; and you shall receive the gift of the Holy Spirit. For the promise is to you and to your children, and to all who are afar off, as many as the Lord our God will call" (Acts 2:38-39).

Peter's message included a call to all three baptisms: repent (salvation), be baptized (water), and receive the gift of the Holy Spirit. It's important to note that the gift of the Holy Spirit is not one particular gift (like healing or prophecy). The gift of the Holy Spirit is *the Holy Spirit* (and **all** the gifts He brings).

Some people say the outpouring of the Holy Spirit was just for the 120 disciples on the Day of Pentecost. However, Jesus told His disciples to "wait for the Promise," which is the baptism in the Holy Spirit. In Acts 2:39, Peter says, "For the promise is to you and to your children, and to all who are afar off, as many as the Lord our God will call." That's us! We get to receive the Holy Spirit too.

In Acts 8, Phillip goes to Samaria to share the Good News of Christ. Verse 12 says:

> But when they believed Philip as he preached the things concerning the kingdom of God and the name of Jesus Christ, both men and women were baptized.

The people got saved and water baptized. Then Peter and John came to visit and "prayed for them that they might receive the Holy Spirit" (v. 15). Many people have been taught that salvation and water-baptism are all that is needed. If that is true, then why would these two apostles pray for people to receive the Holy Spirit? If the new believers already had the Holy Spirit, why does verse 17 say, "Then they laid hands on them, and they received the Holy Spirit"?

Many believers have been saved and water-baptized but have not received the Holy Spirit. Did you receive Jesus as your Lord and Savior? If so, you opened your heart to Him and accepted all He has for you. Why would you not receive the Holy Spirit the same way? You may think you already received Him at salvation. It is true that the Holy Spirit comes to live inside you when you get saved. However, Jesus wants to baptize (or anoint) us with the Holy Spirit.

In Acts 19:2, Paul asks some new disciples in Ephesus, "Did you receive the Holy Spirit when you believed?" If we automatically received the Holy Spirit at salvation, then why would Paul ask this? These disciples did not know anything about the Holy Spirit. They had been baptized "into John's baptism" (v. 3), representing salvation. Paul's response was:

> "John indeed baptized with a baptism of repentance, saying to the people that they should believe on Him who would come after him, that is, on Christ Jesus" (v. 4).

The disciples were then water-baptized, and "when Paul had laid hands on them, the Holy Spirit came upon them, and they spoke with tongues and prophesied" (Acts 19:6). This story follows the New Testament pattern of salvation, water baptism, and Spirit baptism.

First John 5:7 says, "For there are three that bear witness in heaven: the Father, the Word, and the Holy Spirit; and these three are one." These three are witnesses to the supernatural that there is a God. This verse refers to Jesus as "the Word," a name for Christ also found in John 1:1 and Revelation 19:13.

Scripture sometimes refers to salvation as blood. Hebrews 9:22 says there is no remission of sin without the shedding of blood. Jesus shed His blood to wash away our sins. 1 John 5:8 continues, "And there are three that bear witness on earth: the Spirit, the water, and the blood; and these three agree as one." These three bear witness to the fact that there is a God in heaven who changes lives. When you get saved, you become a new person. When you get baptized in water, the old person is cut off. And when you get baptized in the Holy Spirit, you get power to walk in the new life. It's a complete work.

In order to go to heaven, you only have to be saved. The thief on the cross never had the opportunity to be baptized in water or the Holy Spirit, but Jesus said, "Today you will be with Me in Paradise" (Luke 23:43). Many believers are saved but never get water baptized or Spirit baptized, so they have no power. Other believers walk an aisle as a child and get water baptized but don't actually submit their will to Christ until later in life. Since they were baptized as a child, they don't think they need to get baptized again. However, water baptism must take place *after* salvation.

First Corinthians 10 says everything in the Old Testament was written for our instruction and to serve as an example to us. Moses was the Israelites' symbol of Christ—he delivered them from bondage like Christ delivers us from bondage. The Bible also uses figurative language; for example, the Holy Spirit is referred to as oil, fire, and the cloud. Remember, the Israelites were led by the cloud by day and the fire by night.

> Moreover, brethren, I do not want you to be unaware that all our fathers were under the cloud, all passed through the sea, all were baptized into Moses in the cloud and in the sea" (1 Corinthians 10:1-2).

The Israelites were baptized into Moses (their type of Christ), the cloud (the Spirit), and the sea (water).

When the Israelites entered the Tabernacle, there were three required steps before entering the Most Holy Place, where God's presence dwelled. First, they had to shed the blood of a spotless lamb on the altar. This represents salvation. Second, they stopped at a laver to wash their hands with water. This represents water baptism. Third, they had to be anointed with oil from a flask. This represents Spirit baptism. All three steps were required to enter God's presence. All three baptisms are required to walk in the full power available to every believer.

NOTES

RECEIVING THE HOLY SPIRIT | 81

TALK

These questions can be used for group discussion or personal reflection.

Question 1
What are the three baptisms? Is the concept of three baptisms new or familiar to you?

_____

_____

_____

_____

Question 2
What is the difference between the baptism *of* the Holy Spirit and the baptism *in* (or *with*) the Holy Spirit?

_____

_____

_____

_____

Question 3
Read Matthew 3:11, Mark 1:8, Luke 3:16, and John 1:33. What is the significance of Spirit baptism appearing in all four gospels?

_____
_____
_____
_____

Question 4
Read 1 Corinthians 10:1-2. How did the Israelites experience the three baptisms?

_____
_____
_____
_____

Question 5
Read Acts 1:4-5 and 2:38-39. How would you respond to someone who says Spirit baptism was only for the disciples of the early Church?

_____
_____
_____
_____

Receiving The Holy Spirit | 83

PRAY

If studying alone, ask the Holy Spirit to reveal the truth about Himself to you. If in a group, take some time to pray for each other as you think about the truths discussed in this session.

EXPLORE

Do you want to go deeper with this teaching? Here are some additional things to think about, pray for, or write about in your journal throughout the next week.

Key Thought
Jesus did not need to be "born again" because He was born right the first time. Jesus was born a child of God, and then He was water baptized and baptized in the Spirit.

If Jesus—the Son of God and the only sinless person to walk this earth—needed these baptisms, why do many Christians stop with salvation?

_____
_____
_____
_____
_____

Key Verses
Matthew 3:11; Mark 1:8; Luke 3:16; John 1:33; Acts 2:37–39;
1 John 5:7–8

What truths stand out to you as you read these verses?

_____

_____

_____

What is the Holy Spirit saying to you through these Scriptures?

_____

_____

_____

Key Question
When you receive salvation, you become a new person. When you experience water baptism, your old self is cut off. What happens when you receive the baptism in the Holy Spirit?

Key Prayer
Father, thank You for loving me so much. Thank You for sending Your Son to save me and for sending the Holy Spirit to empower me. Jesus, I ask You to baptize me in the Holy Spirit. I cannot walk in victory on my own. Holy Spirit, I submit every part of my life to You. Use me to be a blessing to others and to point them to the Father. In Jesus' name, Amen.

LEADER'S GUIDE

The *Words: Life or Death* Leader's Guide is designed to help you lead your small group or class through the *Words: Life or Death* curriculum. Use this guide along with the curriculum for a life-changing, interactive experience.

BEFORE YOU MEET
- Ask God to prepare the hearts and minds of the people in your group. Ask Him to show you how to encourage each person to integrate the principles all of you discover into your daily lives through group discussion and writing in your journals.
- Preview the video segment for the week.
- Plan how much time you'll give to each portion of your meeting (see the suggested schedule below). In case you're unable to get through all of the activities in the time you have planned, here is a list of the most important questions (from the **Talk** section) for each week.

SUGGESTED SMALL GROUP SCHEDULE
1. **Engage** and **Recap** (5 Minutes)
2. **Watch** or **Read** (20 Minutes)
3. **Talk** (25 Minutes)
4. **Pray** (10 minutes)

SESSION ONE

Q: Why does the quality of your life depend on the words you speak?

Q: Read Romans 10:9. Why does salvation involve your mouth and not just your heart?

SESSION TWO

Q: As a believer, do you have the "right" to say whatever you want? Why or why not?

Q: Read Romans 12:17-18. How should you respond when someone speaks hurtful words over you? How is this different from your natural response?

SESSION THREE

Q: If God is omnipresent, why does Isaiah 59 say He *will not* hear our prayers when we sin?

Q: What are the two keys to tearing down strongholds?

SESSION FOUR

Q: According to James 1:26, why should you bridle your tongue?

Q: Why is a rudder important for ships in good weather? How does this relate to the tongue?

SESSION FIVE

Q: Read James 1:19. Why is it important to be "slow to speak"?

Q: Why should Christians let their hearts tell their minds what to say?

SESSION SIX

Q: What myths have you believed about speaking in tongues?

Q: Read 1 Corinthians 14:14-17. What is the difference between praying with the understanding and praying with the spirit? Why is it important to do both?

SESSION SEVEN

Q: What is the difference between the baptism *of* the Holy Spirit and the baptism *in* (or *with*) the Holy Spirit?

Q: Read Acts 1:4-5 and 2:38-39. How would you respond to someone who says Spirit-baptism was only for the disciples of the early Church?

Remember, the goal is not necessarily to get through all of the questions. The highest priority is for the group to learn and engage in a dynamic discussion.

HOW TO USE THE CURRICULUM

This study has a simple design.

The One Thing
This is a single statement under each session title that sums up the main point—the key idea—of the session.

Recap
Recap the previous week's session, inviting members to share about any opportunities they have encountered throughout the week that apply to what they learned (this doesn't apply to the first week).

Engage
Ask the icebreaker question to help get people talking and feeling comfortable with one another.

Watch
Watch the videos (recommended).

Read
If you're unable to watch the videos, read these sections.

Talk
Discuss the questions.

Pray
Pray together.

Explore
Encourage members to complete the written portion in their books before the next meeting.

KEY TIPS FOR THE LEADER

- Generate participation and discussion.
- Resist the urge to teach. The goal is for great conversation that leads to discovery.
- Ask open-ended questions—questions that can't be answered with "yes" or "no" (e.g., "What do you think about that?" rather than "Do you agree?")
- When a question arises, ask the group for their input first, instead of immediately answering it yourself.
- Be comfortable with silence. If you ask a question and no one responds, rephrase the question and wait for a response. Your primary role is to create an environment where people feel comfortable to be themselves and participate, not to provide the answers to all of their questions.
- Ask the group to pray for each other from week to week, especially about key issues that arise during your group time. This is how you begin to build authentic community and encourage spiritual growth within the group.

KEYS TO A DYNAMIC SMALL GROUP

Relationships
Meaningful, encouraging relationships are the foundation of a dynamic small group. Teaching, discussion, worship, and prayer are important elements of a group meeting, but the depth of each element is often dependent upon the depth of the relationships among members.

Availability
Building a sense of community within your group requires members to prioritize their relationships with one another. This means being available to listen, care for one another, and meet each other's needs.

Mutual Respect
Mutual respect is shown when members value each other's opinions (even when they disagree) and are careful never to put down or embarrass others in the group (including their spouses, who may or may not be present).

Openness
A healthy small group environment encourages sincerity and transparency. Members treat each other with grace in areas of weakness, allowing each other room to grow.

Confidentiality
To develop authenticity and a sense of safety within the group, each member must be able to trust that things discussed within the group will not be shared outside the group.

Shared Responsibility
Group members will share the responsibility of group meetings by using their God-given abilities to serve at each gathering. Some may greet, some may host, some may teach, etc. Ideally, each person should be available to care for others as needed.

Sensitivity
Dynamic small groups are born when the leader consistently seeks and is responsive to the guidance of the Holy Spirit, following His leading throughout the meeting as opposed to sticking to the "agenda." This guidance is especially important during the discussion and ministry time.

Fun!
Dynamic small groups take the time to have fun. Create an atmosphere for fun and be willing to laugh at yourself every now and then!

ABOUT THE AUTHOR

Robert Morris is the founding senior pastor of Gateway Church, a multicampus church in the Dallas/Fort Worth Metroplex. Since it began in 2000, the church has grown to more than 39,000 active members. His television program is aired in over 190 countries, and his radio feature, *Worship & the Word with Pastor Robert*, airs on radio stations across America. He serves as chancellor of The King's University and is the best-selling author of numerous books, including *The Blessed Life*, *The God I Never Knew*, *Truly Free*, and *Frequency*. Robert and his wife, Debbie, have been married 38 years and are blessed with one married daughter, two married sons, and nine grandchildren.

The Blessed Life
ROBERT MORRIS

Too often, greed and materialism can choke out the true spirit of generosity found only in Christ. In this new, revised edition of *The Blessed Life*—featuring fresh stories, illustrations, and testimonials—Robert Morris, founding senior pastor of Gateway Church, examines the true meaning of the blessed life. The enemy wants to keep you from discovering God's principles governing financial stewardship, giving, and blessing. Why? Because once you do, it will change every area of your life from your marriage to your health and finances. It will also impact the kingdom of God.

Book: 978-0-996566-24-7
DVD Message Series: 20150223-DS
Study Guide (Companion to DVD):
978-0-997429-84-8

The Blessed Life resources can be found at the **Gateway Bookstore**.

Did you love using this study guide to dive deeper into *Words: Life or Death*? Then check out these other companion study guides by Robert Morris.

ISBN: 978-1-945529-54-2

The Holy Spirit can be misinterpreted as confusing, controversial, and weird.

People often see the Holy Spirit as an "it" and don't believe Him to be a person who can be understood and welcomed.

The Holy Spirit wants to have a relationship with you. These sessions will help you to recognize the Holy Spirit as a person, develop a connection with Him, and embrace His power to walk in a new life.

ISBN: 978-1-945529-55-9

Do you feel like God is distant and uninvolved in your life?

Do you hide from His presence until you fix your issues?

God has given you everything you need to live in His presence right now!

These sessions will help you change the way you think about your relationship with God and start walking with Him, regardless of your circumstances.

You can find these study guides at the **Gateway Bookstore.**

NOTES